TAKING ACTION
TO ACHIEVE EQUALITY

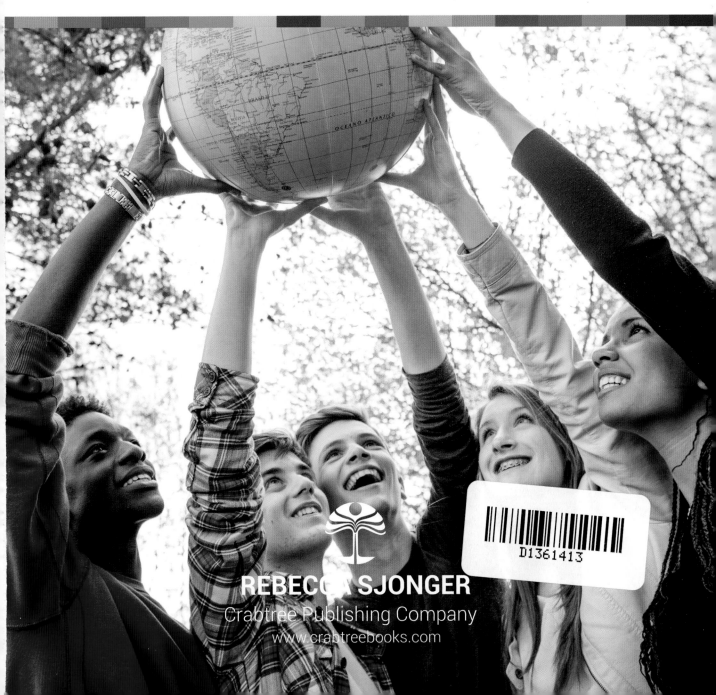

REBECCA SJONGER

Crabtree Publishing Company

www.crabtreebooks.com

D1361413

UN SUSTAINABLE DEVELOPMENT GOALS

Author: Rebecca Sjonger

Series research and development:
Janine Deschenes
Reagan Miller

Editorial director:
Kathy Middleton

Editor: Janine Deschenes

Proofreader and indexer:
Wendy Scavuzzo

Design and photo research:
Katherine Berti

Print and production coordinator:
Katherine Berti

Images:

iStock
fstop123 p. 23b

Shutterstock
CRS PHOTO front cover tl; Vlad Karavaev p. 6bl; davide
bonaldo p. 8tr; Supannee_Hickman p. 8b; paul prescott p.
9br; Ernesto Martin p. 11 br; KMH Photovideo p. 12; Dietmar
Temps p. 13; Stephane Bidouze p. 14; Ravi Shekhar Pandey
p. 16t; CatherineLProd p. 16b; rblfmr p. 17b; klenger p. 20t;
hikrcn p. 21b; John Gomez p. 22; Kelli Hayden p. 25br

Wikimedia Commons
J.Marchand front cover bl; AMD Global p 10b; UNESCO, D.
Willetts p. 27b

All other images from Shutterstock

All dollar amounts in this book are in U.S. funds, unless otherwise indicated.

Library and Archives Canada Cataloguing in Publication

Title: Taking action to achieve equality / Rebecca Sjonger.
Names: Sjonger, Rebecca, author.
Description: Series statement: UN sustainable development goals | Includes index.
Identifiers: Canadiana (print) 2019013397X | Canadiana (ebook) 20190134011 |
ISBN 9780778766629 (softcover) |
ISBN 9780778766582 (hardcover) |
ISBN 9781427124043 (HTML)
Subjects: LCSH: Equality—Juvenile literature. | LCSH: Social justice—Juvenile literature.
Classification: LCC HM821 .S56 2019 | DDC j305—dc23

Library of Congress Cataloging-in-Publication Data

Names: Sjonger, Rebecca, author.
Title: Taking action to achieve equality / Rebecca Sjonger.
Description: New York : Crabtree Publishing Company, [2020] |
Series: UN sustainable development goals | Includes bibliographical references and index.
Identifiers: LCCN 2019029580 (print) | LCCN 2019029581 (ebook) |
ISBN 9780778766582 (hardcover) |
ISBN 9780778766629 (paperback) |
ISBN 9781427124043 (ebook)
Subjects: LCSH: Sustainable Development Goals--Juvenile literature. | Equality--Juvenile
literature. | Economic development--Developing countries--Juvenile literature. | Social
action--International cooperation--Juvenile literature.
Classification: LCC HM821 .S569 2020 (print) | LCC HM821 (ebook) |
DDC 305--dc23
LC record available at https://lccn.loc.gov/2019029580
LC ebook record available at https://lccn.loc.gov/2019029581

Crabtree Publishing Company

www.crabtreebooks.com   1-800-387-7650

Printed in the U.S.A./082019/CG20190712

Published in Canada
Crabtree Publishing
616 Welland Ave.
St. Catharines, Ontario
L2M 5V6

Published in the United States
Crabtree Publishing
PMB 59051
350 Fifth Avenue, 59th Floor
New York, New York 10118

Published in the United Kingdom
Crabtree Publishing
Maritime House
Basin Road North, Hove
BN41 1WR

Published in Australia
Crabtree Publishing
Unit 3–5 Currumbin Court
Capalaba
QLD 4157

CONTENTS

EQUALITY AND THE
SUSTAINABLE DEVELOPMENT GOALS

Do you think everyone should be treated the same? The basic freedoms all people should have are called human rights.

Human rights allow you to share an opinion or go to school, for example. However, they are not always respected. When a person's human rights are not respected, they might be subjected to violence, **oppression**, discrimination, or **exclusion**. Discrimination is unfair treatment based on age, gender, or race. Human rights are threatened by social inequality. This occurs when some people have more power, opportunities, or money than others have.

The Universal Declaration of Human Rights (UDHR) *is a set of rights that everyone around the world has—or should have—because they are human.*

GET TO KNOW THE ISSUE
INEQUALITY AT WORK

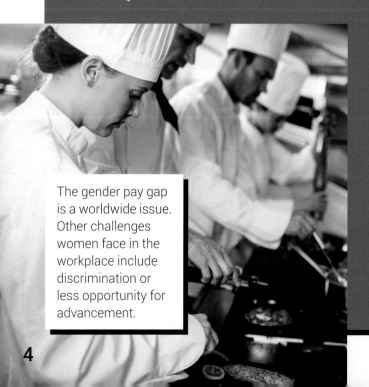

The gender pay gap is a worldwide issue. Other challenges women face in the workplace include discrimination or less opportunity for advancement.

Sam and Chris have a lot in common. These friends live next door to each other. They are in the same classes in junior high. When a local restaurant was hiring, they both got jobs there. Sam and Chris have the same role and do the same tasks. They work the same number of hours each week. But when they get their first paychecks, Chris makes $100 whereas Sam makes $68. There is only one big difference between them: Sam is a girl and Chris is a boy. Sam is treated unfairly because of her gender. This inequality is common around the world. In 2018, females earned about 68 percent of what males earned.

THE UNITED NATIONS

Achieving equality in areas such as the gender pay gap is just one of the missions of the United Nations (UN). This organization includes 193 countries. Together, they promote peace and improve human rights. Their work focuses on global sustainable development. This growth meets the needs of today while ensuring the needs of the future can also be met.

2030 AGENDA
FOR SUSTAINABLE DEVELOPMENT

In September 2015, world leaders met at the UN's headquarters in New York City. They approved an action plan called the 2030 Agenda for Sustainable Development. Its goal is to help people around the world live well while also looking after the planet. The purpose of the agenda is to:

- **End poverty so everyone can afford their basic needs**

- **Increase** economic growth

- **Improve access to jobs, health care, and education**

- **Reduce** climate change and protect people from its impact

The UN was formed after the Second World War to maintain peace and tackle global issues.

GOALS THAT HELP

The agenda centers on 17 Sustainable Development Goals (SDGs). The goals must balance economic growth, the environment, and social issues. They help shape a fair world in which no one is left behind. Many of the SDGs refer to **vulnerable** people. This group includes children, elderly people, pregnant women, people who are ill, and those who live in poverty. They are most at risk when an unexpected event disrupts their lives.

The UN launched the SDGs on January 1, 2016.

GET TO KNOW THE ISSUE
WHY ARE THE SDGS IMPORTANT?

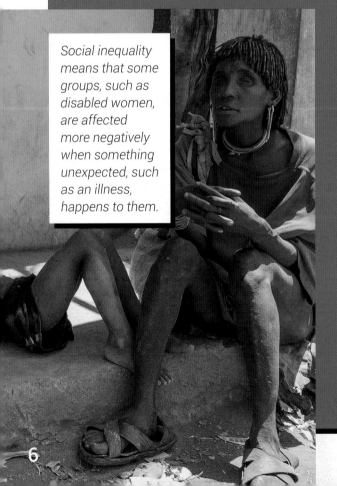

Social inequality means that some groups, such as disabled women, are affected more negatively when something unexpected, such as an illness, happens to them.

Selam is a young woman living in Ethiopia. Droughts have made life hard on her family's small farm. They only have enough money to send one child to school. At first, Selam went. She stopped once her brother was old enough to attend. Then she stayed home and took care of her younger sisters. They lived together in a crowded home. There was no clean water or soap to wash their hands. When one of the children got **trachoma**, Selam was infected, too. Over time, her eyes began to itch, and the pain grew. There was no health care nearby to treat her. Her eyelashes turned inward and damaged her eyeballs. A simple surgery could have helped her. However, Selam's family could not afford to send her away to get it. Plus, they needed her help at home. Selam slowly lost her eyesight. Things could have gone differently for Selam. Her future may have been much brighter if she lived somewhere with less poverty, better access to **sanitation** and health care, and free education for all.

CONNECTED GOALS

This book focuses on how Goals 4, 5, 10, and 16 help achieve equality. (To learn more about these SDGs, flip to page 14.) All 17 of the SDGs fit together and depend on one another. For example, success with improving equality will help provide decent work for all. This supports the end of poverty, which allows for zero hunger, good health and well-being, and so on.

WORKING TOGETHER

People around the world must collaborate to meet these goals. The UN especially wants young people to collaborate on the SDGs. The goals have a much better chance of being met with your support. When you are an adult in 2030, what kind of world do you want to live in? You can play a role in shaping it now!

To collaborate means to work with another person or group to achieve the same purpose.

EQUALITY
ISSUES

Inequality affects many areas of life. People may face discrimination based on their abilities, age, gender, income, social class, race, or religion.

*Four out of five people with disabilities live in **developing countries**, where they have less access to health care.*

More than one billion people live with some kind of **disability**. In addition to their physical or mental challenges, they often have less access to jobs, housing, transportation, and other basics. This unfair treatment can affect their well-being. The obstacles are even greater if they are female, elderly, or part of a **minority group**. Some countries are improving the treatment of people with disabilities. But there is still much work to be done.

*Communities can improve their treatment of people with disabilities by offering **accessible** public transportation.*

DIFFERENT WORLDS

Half of the planet's population lives in cities. However, they do not all have access to the same things. Inequality based on income is a huge problem. People who can afford to live in a city usually have things such as electricity, indoor plumbing, and public transportation. These are just a few examples of **infrastructure** that makes life safer and easier. Those who do not have enough money to buy or rent homes may end up living in a **slum**. Over time, slums become crowded with thousands of people. Slums often lack basic services, including toilets and clean water. This inequality is changing in some areas, however. In about two-thirds of countries that report this data, the poorest half of citizens have the fastest growing incomes. This means more people have basic services, **nutritious** foods, education, and health care.

EXTREME POVERTY

Income inequality is also clear when comparing countries. Extreme poverty affects about 1 in 10 people. They have less than $1.90 to spend each day. Over 40 percent of Africans in the **sub-Saharan region** struggle with extreme poverty. In Central Asia and Europe, the rate is under three percent. The good news is that poverty levels are lower than ever before in history. But its effects are still devastating. One child under the age of 15 dies about every five seconds. Often, this is the result of preventable causes such as dirty drinking water. Children in the poorest one-fifth of the world's population are three times more likely to die before the age of five than those who live in the richest areas.

Children go to school in this slum in India—but schools in slums are usually overcrowded, lacking resources, and in need of repairs.

THINK DEEP

Have you noticed any differences in how people live in different areas of your community?

What do you think could be some of the reasons for these differences?

GENDER ROLES

For thousands of years, men have mainly held power. The roles women and men play today still show inequality worldwide. Being male or female is biological, or the way someone is born. This is called their sex. Gender is the social characteristics that people learn as they grow up. Someone's gender relates to how they view masculinity and femininity, and how they view themselves. Some people's gender does not match their biological sex. They are a very vulnerable group. In some places, their lives are at risk because of discrimination. Many women are also exposed to violence because of the imbalance of power. Traditional beliefs about gender limit their rights in some countries.

WHO RUNS THE WORLD?

Girls and women make up half the world's population. However, they are not half of the workforce. More than two-thirds of business leaders are men. Under 25 percent of national government leaders are women. Inequality starts when girls are born. Globally, they get fewer nutritious foods. They also get less health care and are more likely to die young. Girls living in Oceania, sub-Saharan Africa, and Western Asia are less likely to go to school. This makes it difficult for them to get decent work. About 37,000 girls under the age of 18 get married each year. This number is much higher than for boys of the same age. Marrying off daughters can help a family living in poverty.

Many people grow up learning that men and women have certain behaviors expected of them. But these expectations can be harmful. How does this image go against an expected gender behavior?

The number of female Chief Executive Officers (CEOs) is much lower than the number of male CEOs. Lisa Su is one example of a female CEO. She leads a technology company.

GENDER EQUALITY

Gender equality is fairness in the opportunities open to men and women. It is a basic human right. Some progress has been made recently. Child marriages are down by about one-third in the last 10 years. About 100 countries track how much their governments spend on gender equality efforts. They know that the SDGs cannot be achieved without fair treatment for all. However, it is difficult to change the way people from diverse societies think.

A PEACEFUL WORLD

The UN's goals can only be met in a world where people are treated equally. **Justice** aims to create fair treatment through a society's ideals and laws. They should not discriminate against anyone. However, in many places around the world, people are treated unfairly because of their **sexual orientation**, religion, or race. Simply sharing their views may put them in danger.

Discrimination and corruption can be found in a variety of **public institutions**. Corruption occurs when people who are in power abuse it and break the law. For example, a police officer may accept money in exchange for covering up a crime. In addition, the **legal system** can be unfair to both guilty and innocent people. About one-third of prisoners around the world are being held without a **sentence**. People who cannot support or protect themselves face higher levels of violence. Children often experience the worst effects. Equality and justice for all ensures the well-being and safety of people worldwide.

Corruption can happen anywhere, including schools, governments, and courts. It results in the unfair and unjust treatment of people.

Prisoners held without sentences have no options but to wait. Sometimes, the prison conditions are very poor. This prison in the Democratic Republic of the Congo was built for 35 people, but held 70.

YOUTH FOR CHANGE

On February 14, 2018, there was a mass shooting at Marjory Stoneman Douglas High School. Afterward, classmates banded together to show their anger over gun violence in the United States. Attention from the media helped them spread their message. One month later, over one million American students joined the March for Our Lives. They walked out of school to urge leaders to make gun laws stricter. The students built a network across the country of people who are fighting violence. They work together to create a peaceful society. This leads toward equality for all.

ORGANIZATION	Never Again movement
ESTABLISHED	2018
ORIGIN	Parkland, Florida
FOCUS	Gun control movement led by young people
INVOLVEMENT	Students across the United States

The students started the Never Again movement, which urges stricter gun laws. To reach this goal, they contact government representatives, hold events, and speak to the media.

DECENT EDUCATION

Education is directly linked to creating a fair and sustainable world. Going to school helps ease poverty, increase gender equality, and promote peace. The number of youth in school is increasing globally. More than 90 percent of children in most developing countries attend primary school. **Literacy rates** are improving, which helps people find work. However, more than 260 million school-aged young people are still not getting an education. More than 50 million are missing out on primary school. They do not learn basic math and reading skills. Over half of those who are not in school live in sub-Saharan Africa. Some of the challenges there include lack of proper schools, and infrastructure, such as power and water. It is difficult to find well-trained teachers, especially in **rural** communities. Places affected by conflicts have a very hard time educating young people. There is still plenty of hope for the future, though. Lifelong learning opportunities are growing. It is never too late to learn basic skills that will help in all aspects of life.

EQUALITY CONNECTIONS

Inequality has an impact on people worldwide. However, the poor and vulnerable are usually the most affected. Taking action to achieve equality plays a huge part in building a world in which no one is left behind. For example, when young people get a quality education (Goal 4), they are more likely to find decent work as adults (Goal 8). This increases their access to food (Goal 2) and health care (Goal 3). These are just a few of the ways that the SDGs connect.

? If quality education is available worldwide, how many more young people will have the skills they need to succeed?

Answer: About one billion

These students attend a small school in a village in Malawi. Student enrollment there has increased, but there is still a lack of teachers, schools, and resources.

THINK DEEP

Do you know who pays for your school building, the teachers, and your supplies?

Why do you think some countries pay for these things in different ways?

How could you find out more?

GOALS
TO ACHIEVE EQUALITY

The 17 SDGs are a joint call for action. Each one has its own targets. They relate to the causes of the issues. A goal is met when all its targets are hit.

To achieve all the SDGs, a total of 169 targets must be reached. Success is measured by one or more indicators, or measurable ways to track progress. Together, the goals, targets, and indicators create a detailed plan for success.

Goal 4 will be met only when all people have equal access to a quality education.

GOAL

4 QUALITY EDUCATION

TARGET

End gender inequality in education and provide equal access to it for vulnerable people

INDICATORS

Even numbers of female and male students from both urban and rural areas and all income levels

As the numbers become more balanced in the example above, the target will be hit. The goal is then a step closer to being met. As each goal is met, it also helps achieve the other goals.

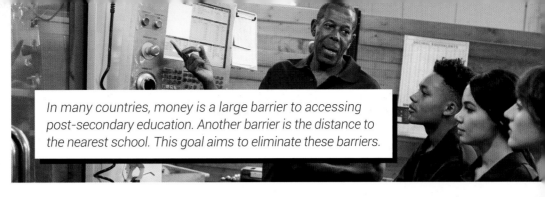

In many countries, money is a large barrier to accessing post-secondary education. Another barrier is the distance to the nearest school. This goal aims to eliminate these barriers.

QUALITY EDUCATION

When young people cannot go to school, it is often because they cannot afford it. That is why one target is free quality education for all. The UN wants everyone to be able to go to primary and secondary school. Success is measured by the number of students enrolled in various grade levels. Strong numbers need to continue through all grades. Equal access to post-secondary education and training is also important. The number of men and women enrolled in training programs, colleges, and universities each year shows if the target is met. This SDG also focuses on lifelong learning. One of its targets ensures that all young people and a greater number of adults can read and do math. An indicator is the percentage of the global population with these skills.

CHALLENGES TO OVERCOME

The roadblocks to education in each country are different. In some cases, war makes it difficult to run schools. In others, there is not enough money to train and hire decent teachers. Developing countries struggle with a lack of infrastructure and school facilities. Youth living in rural areas may live far from a school. Another major issue is gender inequality. Over 100 million girls around the world do not go to school. Often, this is because they are not seen as being as important as boys.

GLOBAL EFFORTS NEEDED

This goal could be met if we:

- **Urge governments to make education a priority**

- **Make primary and secondary school free for everyone**

- **Encourage businesses to support post-secondary education and training in innovative ways**

- **Make girls and boys equal**

Some families need children to work and cannot send them to school. Working toward goals to end poverty can help achieve Goal 4.

In India, the literacy rate for females is far lower than the rate for males. Views on gender there mean that fewer females receive a quality education. Many must stay at home with their families, and marry young.

YOUTH FOR CHANGE

Amresh Mishra attended the Indian Institute of Technology in the 1990s. Children from nearby slums were often around looking for food. He started the organization Kartavya to help them get an education. Over time, it grew to offer many services to help youth living in poverty. Young volunteers adopt a local community. They help provide study centers and libraries, offer skills development, and arrange for health care.

ORGANIZATION	Kartavya
ESTABLISHED	1999
ORIGIN	Dhanbad, India
FOCUS	Helps educate children in India and improve their quality of life
INVOLVEMENT	College and university students across India

Amresh and the Kartavya volunteers hope to educate a generation of youth in India who can succeed and pass on knowledge.

5 GENDER EQUALITY

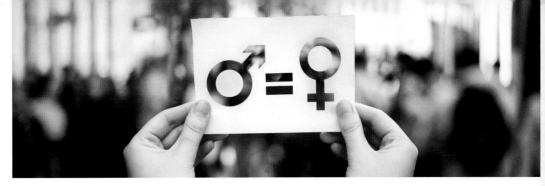

GENDER EQUALITY

Girls and women need equality in many areas addressed by the SDGs. This includes quality education, access to health care, and inclusion and safety in the workplace. A big target of this goal is to end all discrimination against girls and women. This is measured in part by whether there are laws in place that focus on this goal. The UN also wants to end all early and forced marriages. One indicator is the number of girls married before the age of 15, and also before they turn 18. Gender equality is achieved only when women and men share power at all levels of leadership. Balancing roles in economic, political, and public life is one target. A way to measure its success is to count the number of women in governments around the world.

GLOBAL EFFORTS NEEDED

The world must make some big changes, including:

- **Improving women's rights in every country**

- **Tackling cultural practices that harm girls and women**

- **Recruiting women for jobs until there is a gender balance in workplaces**

CHALLENGES TO OVERCOME

According to the **World Economic Forum**, it will take decades to close the pay gap. Western Europe may have pay equality by the year 2079. But North America is falling behind. It could take more than 160 years to get gender equality there. Not everyone is pushing for progress. Cultural practices in some places make change difficult. Women who do not get an education, who live in poverty, or who are vulnerable in other ways find it hard to get ahead.

People raise awareness of the pay gap on Equal Pay Day. In 2019, it was held on April 2. See page 25 to learn more about the day it is held.

17

The Youth for Gender Equality participatants want to create a world in which every person's voice is heard.

YOUTH FOR
CHANGE

Plan Canada, the Canadian Teachers' Federation, and other partners empower youth in the Youth for Gender Equality program. The youth come from diverse backgrounds, including young people who are **2SLGBTQIA+**, **Indigenous**, or new to Canada. They live in rural and urban communities. The program helps them find solutions to end discrimination. Their efforts are by youth and for youth. They work together to achieve Goal 5 in all areas of life.

ORGANIZATION	Youth for Gender Equality
ESTABLISHED	2019
ORIGIN	Canada
FOCUS	Engages youth in tackling gender equality issues
INVOLVEMENT	More than 300 young people across Canada

27 youth participants created a "roadmap" for success. It lays out the actions they will take to achieve their goals. One action is to promote STEM programs for girls.

10 REDUCED INEQUALITIES

All people must be included in social, economic, and political settings.

REDUCED INEQUALITIES

All people in all places deserve to be treated equally. One target that helps meet this goal is to grow the incomes of the bottom 40 percent of the world's population. The growth must be at a higher rate than other groups to achieve equality by 2030. The UN also wants to ensure all people have equal opportunity and are treated equally under the law. This is measured by the number of people who reported an experience of discrimination or harassment—one which fits under international human rights laws. Another target promotes the safe, orderly movement of people who leave their homes to find work in other countries. One indicator is the number of countries that have useful policies, or plans and rules, in place to help them.

CHALLENGES TO OVERCOME

A major roadblock is that inequality is the norm around the world. It also has widespread impacts. These include poverty, hunger, lack of health and well-being, and so many more issues. For there to be progress, attitudes toward equality need to change. All people must learn to care for others as they do themselves.

GLOBAL EFFORTS NEEDED

This goal requires some serious effort, such as:

- **Ending discrimination at all levels, from government policies to one-on-one relations between people**

- **Supporting the efforts of developing countries to find innovative solutions that work well for them**

- **Viewing everyone on the planet as equally important**

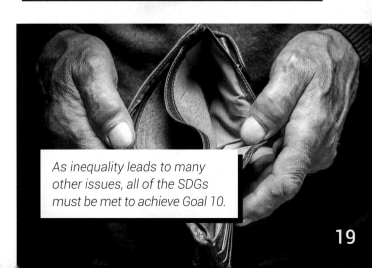

As inequality leads to many other issues, all of the SDGs must be met to achieve Goal 10.

In a safe, fair society, people feel comfortable and protected in their communities.

PEACE, JUSTICE, AND STRONG INSTITUTIONS

When a society is not fair or free of violence, there is a never-ending cycle of conflict. The UN wants to stop these struggles all over the planet. A major target is to lower violence in all its forms everywhere. This is measured in part by the number of people who feel safe walking alone in their neighborhood. This SDG aims to create public services that are responsible and useful for all people. When a certain percentage of the population is satisfied with these institutions, the target will be met. Another target encourages the rule of law and equal justice for all. One indicator is a lower number of people who are in prisons, but do not have a formal sentence.

CHALLENGES TO OVERCOME

Human rights are ignored and abused in every country. In some, human rights violations are openly supported by the government. For example, almost one million ethnic Uighur people have been held captive in "re-education" camps in China. They are not criminals. Instead, they are Muslims being forced to embrace Chinese culture instead of their own traditions. There are many other instances of injustice worldwide. Corruption is especially hard to end when police forces and courts are part of it.

GLOBAL EFFORTS NEEDED

What could people around the world do?

- **Fight abuses of human rights in every country**

- **Create a global** birth registry **to help keep track of vulnerable young people**

- **Call out global leaders whose actions do not line up with this SDG**

*Many legal **asylum-seekers** are detained in overcrowded centers at the U.S. border.*

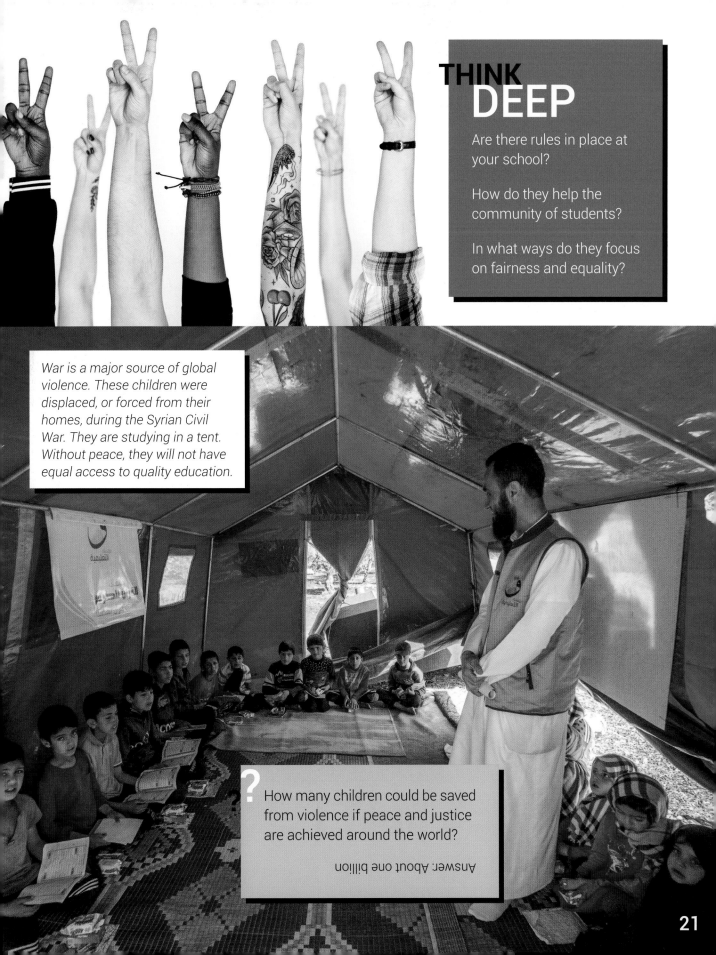

War is a major source of global violence. These children were displaced, or forced from their homes, during the Syrian Civil War. They are studying in a tent. Without peace, they will not have equal access to quality education.

? How many children could be saved from violence if peace and justice are achieved around the world?

Answer: About one billion

When the UN created the SDGs, it was only the beginning. Everyone from world leaders to kids in schools must work together to put these plans into action. People all over the planet need to do their part. Young people can get involved in many ways. You can take the lead as a change-maker and innovator!

BETTER TOGETHER

If people collaborate, we can get more done than we could on our own. Sharing resources allows us to make a bigger impact. We can pool things such as skills, knowledge, tools, time, and money. Multiple groups can join together to help a community—or change the world! For example, The Movement for Black Lives (M4BL) brings together more than 50 groups from all over the United States. These groups, such as Black Youth Project 100, collaborate to address the **racism**, social inequality, and justice issues. The Community Justice Network for Youth and other organizations are not part of M4BL, but support it by **endorsing** some of its efforts. Each group plays a part in making the country a better place for black citizens— a group that is not treated fairly.

Black Lives Matter is an organization that is part of M4BL.

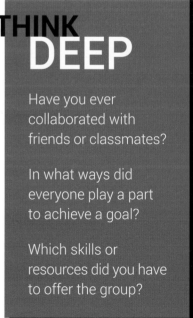

THINK
DEEP

Have you ever collaborated with friends or classmates?

In what ways did everyone play a part to achieve a goal?

Which skills or resources did you have to offer the group?

We all need to find a way to support the SDGs!

Sending trained teachers is one way to help disabled youth access education. Building accessible hallways, rooms, and entrances is another.

A GLOBAL TEAM

The diverse countries that form the UN are working together to meet the SDGs. Each one has its own plans to meet the commitments it has made. But to be successful, they need help. All levels of government need to take the lead. Civil society organizations (CSOs) do their part by bringing together people with a shared interest in helping the public. These groups do not make a profit and are not run by governments. Businesses can also help meet the goals.

START SMALL, THINK BIG

In 1985, a school in London, England, sent students to work as international supply teachers. Over the years, the program became known as Restless Development. It grew to include volunteers helping closer to home. There are now more than 1,000 young people making a difference in more than 10 countries. They collaborate with CSOs, businesses, and governments. These supporters help fund and carry out a wide variety of programs. More than 200 of their partnerships are youth-led. Volunteers work with local groups and communities on projects that help achieve equality and improve human rights. For example, Restless Development partnered with Nzeve Deaf Children's Centre in Zimbabwe. This collaboration helped improve disability inclusion by training people to work with deaf youth. Each small action helps meet the overall goals.

TAKING ACTION
WORLDWIDE

Global citizens are working hard to achieve equality. These are people who understand that world issues affect everyone. They are collaborating to achieve all the SDGs by 2030.

Global citizens work with others in their communities, their countries, and around the world to tackle specific targets. Every effort in every area helps create a fairer, more sustainable world.

THINK DEEP

Do you think doing something to meet the SDGs in your community could help make a difference in the wider world?

Why or why not?

MARK YOUR
CALENDAR

Global action days are created by the UN and many other groups. They bring attention to important issues. The public is engaged through education programs, community projects, and fundraising efforts. Have you ever taken part in any of the following examples?

JANUARY 24
INTERNATIONAL DAY OF EDUCATION

An awareness program urges world leaders to make quality education available to all young people.

MARCH 21
INTERNATIONAL DAY FOR THE ELIMINATION OF RACIAL DISCRIMINATION

On March 21, 1960, police shot and killed 69 protestors fighting apartheid in South Africa. It is now called the Sharpeville Massacre. The UN declared this as a day of remembrance that also challenges racism.

SEPTEMBER 21
PEACE DAY

People around the world join in a variety of events to promote peace, such as hosting community meals or observing a minute of silence at noon. They also hold marches and parades.

NOVEMBER 25 TO DECEMBER 10
16 DAYS OF ACTIVISM

This longer event raises awareness to end violence against women. It begins on the International Day for the Elimination of Violence Against Women. It ends on International Human Rights Day. These two action days are purposely linked together because the issues are connected.

DATE MOVES EACH YEAR
EQUAL PAY DAY

Each year, the date reveals how many extra days women had to work to make the same amount as men the year before.

You do not have to wait until a specific day to take action!

25

SOCIAL ENTREPRENEURS

One way that young change-makers can solve social issues is by starting their own businesses. **Social enterprises** can address any of the SDGs. For example, brothers Craig and Marc Kielburger started ME to WE in 2008. It sells items such as jewelry, which is made by people around the world. This helps the economies in developing countries. As more goods are made and sold, people make more money and their quality of life improves. ME to WE also runs global cultural education trips for youth, families, and businesses. Their Take Action camps build up young leaders. All these efforts help fund the WE Charity. It partners with communities in Latin America, Asia, and Africa. Together, they form WE Villages. These communities use sustainable solutions to tackle challenges. For instance, they provide quality education, lower the number of children who work instead of going to school, and fight gender inequality.

Starting your own social enterprise can also help achieve Goal 8: Decent work and economic growth.

? How old will you be in 2030?

Answer: Do the math!

26

YOUTH FOR CHANGE

A worker at the Kakuma Refugee Camp in Kenya asked Belgian educator Koen Timmers for help. At the time, there were about 180,000 people living in the camp. Schools set up for the children had up to 200 students in their classes! They did not have the resources to provide a quality education. Timmers arranged for computers and Internet connections. This allows teachers from around the world to give video lessons to the refugee students. Students from their own classrooms can also connect with the refugees. Both groups have the chance to learn from each other.

ORGANIZATION	Kakuma Project
ESTABLISHED	2015
ORIGIN	Kakuma, Kenya, and Hasselt, Belgium
FOCUS	Educating refugee children
INVOLVEMENT	About 350 educators in 70 countries

The Kakuma Project helps refugee students access better education by connecting them with qualified teachers. It also helps student participants around the world understand inequality and support others.

YOU CAN
DO IT!

There are more youth on Earth than ever before—almost two billion! Each young person has the power to make a difference in the world. What could you do?

REFLECT

• Which issues or projects in this book interested you the most? Learn more about them!

• What talents or skills could you share with others?

• What could the world look like in 2030 if the SDGs are achieved? What if they are not?

You do not have to be part of the UN to create an awesome action plan!

ACTION PLAN

What is one action you could take today to help achieve equality? Check out some of the ideas on this page to help inspire you.

FUTURE GOALS

Working toward sustainable development will not end in 2030. The global efforts to meet the UN's goals will need to continue. The SDGs were based on an earlier plan called the Millennium Development Goals. These eight goals looked at poverty, education, social equality, health, the environment, and global partnerships. They began in 2000. In 2030, the UN will look at the progress that has been made. It will need to find ways to keep up with its successes. It will also need to learn from areas that fall short. The youth of today will be the leaders who decide on the next steps in the future!

4 QUALITY EDUCATION	• Research education in different countries, then raise people's awareness • Find out what your rights are as a student
5 GENDER EQUALITY	• Speak out against sexist words or actions • Make friends with girls and boys to help build understanding and respect
10 REDUCED INEQUALITIES	• Support stores that give part of their profits to charities that help people in need • Share social media posts that educate people about equality
16 PEACE, JUSTICE AND STRONG INSTITUTIONS	• Learn about a culture that is different from your own • Promote peaceful actions at home and at school • Always report bullying to a trusted adult

LEARN MORE

WEBSITES

Find out more about all the Sustainable Development Goals: **www.youneedtoknow.ch**

Check out the Girls Get Equal movement: **https://plan-international.org/girls-get-equal**

Learn about WE Villages described on page 26: **https://bit.ly/2S09NXu**

Read the *Young Person's Guide: Changing the World Edition*: **https://bit.ly/2McwYOT**

FURTHER READING

Ellis, Deborah. *The Breadwinner Trilogy*. Groundwood Books, 2009.

Park, Linda Sue. *A Long Walk to Water*. Clarion Books, 2012.

Yousafzai, Malala, and Patricia McCormick. *I Am Malala: How One Girl Stood Up for Education and Changed the World (Young Readers Edition)*. Little, Brown Books for Young Readers, 2016.

ACTIVITIES

Play the Go Goals! downloaded board game: **https://go-goals.org**

Start an SDG Book Club: **https://bit.ly/32g35Bq**

Get inspired by 170 daily actions to transform our world: **https://bit.ly/2LGK9Un**

GLOSSARY

2SLGBTQIA+ Two-Spirit, lesbian, gay, bisexual, transgender, queer and questioning, intersex, and asexual

accessible Able to be used or reached by people of all abilities

asylum-seekers People who seek protection in a new country

birth registry A written record of children born in a country

climate change The gradual change in Earth's usual weather. Usually refers to global warming, or the gradual increase in Earth's average temperature, caused by human activity.

developing countries Countries with fewer industries and a lower Human Development Index, which measures such things as life expectancy, income, and education

disability A mental or physical condition that limit's a person's ability to do some tasks

economic growth An increase in the number of goods made and services provided

endorsing Stating approval or support of something

exclusion Leaving someone out or not allowing them to participate in something

Indigenous Native to or originally from a place

infrastructure The systems, services, and facilities that help a society operate

justice Fair and impartial treatment

legal system In a country, the procedure for enforcing the law

literacy rate The percentage of the population who can read and write

minority group A cultural, ethnic, or racial group that is smaller in number than the dominant group

nutritious Containing substances that encourage growth and good health

oppression Cruel or unjust treatment by those in power

public institutions Places paid for by governments and used by the public, such as a library

racism The belief that some races are superior to others and that people of certain races have specific traits

rural Relating to the country

sanitation Systems for cleaning dirty water and disposing of waste

sentence Official punishment for a crime, given in a court

sexual orientation The gender to which a person is attracted

slum A run-down, crowded urban area. Many people in slums live in poverty.

social enterprises A business that raises money for social causes

sub-Saharan region The region of Africa below the Sahara Desert

trachoma An eye infection that can cause blindness

vulnerable Easily hurt or affected by something

World Economic Forum An international organization that aims to improve the global economy

INDEX

ABOUT THE AUTHOR

Rebecca Sjonger is the author of more than 50 books for young people. She recommends the many resources created by the United Nations. They are a great starting point to learn more about the Sustainable Development Goals!